DAILY STEPS TO RENEWAL

Daily Steps to Renewal

Casey Treat

ISBN 1-57921-073-2
LCCN 97-62128

Daily Steps to Renewal

Published by Christian Faith International
PO Box 98800
Seattle, WA 98198

Contents

Introduction

You are a person created in the likeness and image of God. This means you have dreams, desires, goals, and visions. You are seeking—seeking a way to be more, to accomplish greater things, to develop deeper relationships. I hope that you are also seeking to have a better relationship with God, our Father.

The way to become a better person is not always easy. Therefore, many people just settle for what they have and assume that there can be nothing better or higher for them. If you let that attitude control you, nothing can bring you to what I call the *next level.* The next level is where you become a more fulfilled person—one who achieves much, gives much, and is able to receive much.

Since you are reading this book, I believe you are seeking God for growth, increase, and change in your life. You desire God's perfect will, and I believe that you can have it because He will give you what you ask for. Nevertheless, you must do your part. God will provide the encouragement, the guidance, the support, and the wisdom, but you need to follow a plan.

When I climbed Mt. Rainier, in Washington State, I had a route to follow that would surely get me to the summit. A small group and I prepared for seven months for this trip. We spent two nights and three days on the mountain, climbing 14,500 feet to the summit.

When I was out driving with my grandfather as a child, he would always point to Mt. Rainier and say, "Look at that mountain." Many weekends we would drive there and stay in a little park somewhere around the mountain, and he would say, "Casey, look at that mountain. Wow, look at that mountain."

I was a little kid, and I was thinking, *What's the big deal? Yeah, it's still there, Grandpa.* Well, it got in me. Somehow, my grandfather affected me—infected me. So now, as a father, I say to my kids, "Look, Micah (or Caleb, or Tasha), at that mountain."

And they talk to me just the way I used to talk to my grandpa, "Yep, it's still there, Dad."

I think my grandfather recognized that the glory, the majesty of the mountain, declared the glory of the Lord, and he put that appreciation in me. And so, from the time I was a small child I looked at that mountain, and finally one day I said, "I'm going to stand on top of that mountain." Now, forty years later, I have finally done it.

A funny thing about climbing a mountain, it seems you are tired the moment you start. You realize right away that the process is going to be long, and it is not going to be fun. But I went through it for the reward of accomplishing a goal and reaching the summit. The first lesson we learned is that you just keep going, take one more step, just keep on keeping on.

How do you have a successful marriage? You take one more step. You talk one more time. You forgive one more time. You accept one more time.

How do you grow a business? You show up for work one more day. You make one more sale. You keep going one more week.

My church, Christian Faith Center, has never done anything fast. We just keep on going. We reach one more person. We send out one more broadcast. We help start one more church. We have one more Sunday service. And that is how you get to the summit—you just take one more step.

Climbing that mountain never got easier. I never got to the place when I felt better. I frequently asked myself, "Casey, why are you doing this?"

One of the things I noticed while climbing that mountain was that there was nobody there but us. Not too many folks will ever see that view. Not too many people will enjoy that place. Likewise, there are a lot of Christians who will never experience a deep, powerful, profound relationship with God. Most are willing to settle for a low level in their relationship with God. A few will climb to the summit. A few will go through the pain. A few will go through the effort. A few will do what it takes to get to the top.

It is so easy to settle into a mundane lifestyle—a routine, a life of just barely making it, a life of getting by, a life of hanging in there. So many people just go through the routine of life.

One of the reasons I wanted to climb Mt. Rainier was because I wanted to get out of my routine. I have a commitment to myself that I will regularly do something I have never done before. I will regularly get out of my comfort zone—my everyday life; my couch-potato, maintenance mentality—and get beyond myself. I will regularly do something that challenges a part of my spirit, soul, and body because I do not want to be the average human.

When was the last time you did something for the first time? When was the last time you found something in yourself that you didn't know was there? When people settle for the easy way, for the maintenance way, for the just-get-by type of lifestyle, we never find out what really is in us. You will never know what you and God can really do until you get to a higher place, until you fight for a higher relationship, until you reach for higher goals, until you press for a higher life. I want to live this way in the Spirit. I want to find out what God can really do with me.

Let me briefly outline the steps that have worked for me and will work for you. As you climb the mountain of life, your rise to the next level starts with **a desire** to go beyond where you are now. If you are happy where you're at—satisfied, fulfilled, and feeling like you have arrived—then maybe you should just put this book away and have a really good day! If you're like me, however—and most people probably are—there is a feeling of never being satisfied. We are content and happy and yet not fulfilled or satisfied, because we don't think we're done.

The best illustration I can give in this area has to do with my children. I'm really content with my nine-year-old, Micah; and I'm happy with where he is in his knowledge, skill, ability and maturity. But I'm not satisfied. He is doing well for a nine-year-old, but I want him to be ten, fifteen and twenty. I'm happy where he is, but I'm not satisfied. I want him to grow up and become more mature.

I feel the same way about my life: I'm content where I am. I'm glad for what I am accomplishing, but I'm not where I want to be yet. So I am going to keep pressing on to grow more, to mature more, to prosper more, to rise to a higher level of success.

So, what are we talking about? It is a simple word: **change.** This concept is easy to talk about, to think about, even to pray about. But it is not always easy to put into action.

Change has been the subject of hundreds, if not thousands, of books, articles, video tapes, and sermons over the years. Organizations face it, churches face it, and individuals face it. There is not one development in human history that could have occurred without it. Anyone who could not, or would not, change has been left behind and has not fulfilled his or her heart's desire.

Think about all the people who clung to their horses and buggies when the automobile came along. They did not want to change to a faster way of travel. Remember the people who laughed at the Wright brothers when they took their primitive "flyer" to Kitty Hawk, North Carolina, and managed to get it to stay in the air for over 100 feet. Change is a way of life, and it is the key to your next level.

Don't practice *habit insanity*. Don't think if you continue to do what you are doing now you will somehow get different results than what you are getting now. A lot of people are deceived by that. They somehow think if they just keep on doing what they're doing, even though it's not working now, someday it's going to work. That's habit insanity.

Change is resisted for several reasons, which we will get into as we go along in this book.

There is another drag on us that often prevents us from getting to another level of life—**lack of confidence** in ourselves. It stems from not accurately assessing what we have already accomplished and how much potential we have for new things.

The next stumbling block to rising to a level of success that we all dream of is **ignorance** of our personal destiny. Destiny is what we are intended to be and to do, as determined by God. It is not a cold, impersonal fate, but an intentional direction for one's life. It is vital to discover this destiny and start contributing planning and energy to reaching it. That is vitally important in getting from where we are now to where we think and believe we should be.

Change is fun and rewarding, but not easy. You must go for it and believe. You can change, grow, and become what God wills for you. You see, much of our dissatisfaction comes from not being what He wants us to be and what we know we can be.

This book will help you to know your destiny by opening up your thoughts to better comprehend God's thoughts. It will go further to show you what you can accomplish in your life. Then, by following it, you will take the steps to make it happen.

To develop the skills necessary to change, we'll walk together through a series of thoughts and decisions. Along the way you will:

- *Decide* what you really want (Luke 10:38–42)
- *Learn* the right way to think (II Tim. 2:15)
- *Speak* the right confessions (Prov. 18:21)
- *Focus* on your destiny (Eph. 1:11)
- *Meditate* on the Word (Josh. 1:8)

- *Be* who you are called to be (Josh. 1:6)
- *Practice* until it is comfortable (Phil. 2:12*b*)

Each step will be introduced with thoughts that I believe will serve you well, along with questions and scripture that will help you focus and keep your mind and spirit on your goal. These questions are meant to be thought provokers and prayer starters, not ultimate questions. You may choose to reflect on each one several times.

Let's go up to the next level!

Planning the Ascent

There must be a strong desire, clear vision and purpose to move forward in change and transformation. Your strength to push through old habits, your energy to keep going when it seems too hard, and your focus to know where you are going depend on these three things: desire, vision, and a sense of destiny.

DESIRE: What do you want for your life?

Desire is a very powerful force. You must want something deeply to go after it. God gives you the desires of your heart as you delight in Him (Ps. 37:4). He uses the force of desire to direct your life and move you toward destiny—His plan for you. There is a reason why you want things that others don't, and other people want things that you don't. It all has to do with God working in you through desires.

Desires are thoughts that create feelings and motivation to do, obtain or accomplish. They are not fantasies, head trips or passing fancies. Desires come from the heart and are strong motivational factors in our lives. Satan and the world would like to pervert your desires to be unnatural, negative and carnal. Then the God-given power of desire is used to accomplish or get negative and ungodly things.

Clarify your desires. When we're young we think we want certain things in life. Then after we try it a little bit we think, *I don't really want that.*

I used to think it was so cool to travel. There was a time when I thought I would have my own pilot's license and have my own airplane for all my traveling. I lost that desire during my third flight in a little Aztec. It was sometime when we were bouncing over Victoria, B.C., or brushing snow off the wings in Alberta. Somewhere in there I decided I'm not interested in this private plane stuff.

Planning the Ascent

But you do have to experience certain things before you really sort out what you desire and what you really want. That's why the Bible says in Matthew 21:22, "And all things, whatever you ask in prayer, believing, you will receive." You get focused on what you really want, then you can focus your faith and you can get it. Most people don't know what they want. What do you really desire? "Well, you know, whatever." "I'm just leaving it up to the Lord." Well, the Lord isn't in control of every aspect of your life. He has given you a will, a mind, and certain parameters in which you can flow in His kingdom and under His plans for your life. What do you want?

I've been in counseling so many times with husbands and wives who are frustrated and mad. Sometimes they are at the point where they want a divorce. They say, "I want out. This marriage will never work."

I'll say, "Why won't it work?"

"Well, I can't stand it anymore; I'm fed up. I'm sick and tired of this relationship."

"Do you want your spouse to change?"

"Yes, yes, I want them to change."

"What do you want them to change?"

"Well, everything, just change everything."

"Well, what do you mean *everything*? You don't like their nose?"

"No, that's not it."

"Well, you said *everything!* You don't like their hair? Their voice?"

"No, that's not what I mean."

"Yes, but you said *everything*; what do you really want?"

"Well, I don't know."

They're going to bail out of the marriage and they don't even know what it would take to save the relationship. Maybe it's very simple, but they don't know what they want. So we can't get any focus on the future because they don't really know what they desire. Clarifying desires is a big part in relationships, business, and career planning. Ask yourself what do you really want, and get a clear picture.

It will really help if you take some time to find out the desires of your heart. What are they? As a preliminary discovery attempt, answer these questions right now—write down the answers as you presently see them.

1. What are the three things you really want changed in your life?
2. What three things do you really want to accomplish in your lifetime?

While some are very clear on the answers to these questions, others will need to spend some time sorting them out. Even though this is just a beginning, meditate on your answers. They are for today, and they are real in you now. It is quite likely that they will change as you walk with me through this material, and that is all right.

Evaluate these responses. Are they yours, rather than those of your friends or perhaps your parents? You have to start where you are, which is a vital requirement for change. It is a baseline, a set of thoughts you put in place to see the progress you make. Imagine a football field without first-down markers. The players, coaches and officials could never tell whether the team had gone anywhere, because there would be no mark to tell where they came from. And imagine the further confusion if there were no goal lines. No one could tell if there was a touchdown!

Evaluate your responses, but don't judge them too harshly. It is possible that you think that one or more are somehow too human, selfish, or even grandiose. Many times we are afraid to think big and go for God's best in life. Let yourself believe God has an abundant life planned for you, and go for it.

Keep your answers in a notebook, because you will need to refer back to them from time to time. They are your three greatest desires for change and your three greatest desires for your future.

VISION: **What will your future look like?**

Now you need to take a second vital step. Begin to picture your future. This is for the time being, an internal picture, one that does not have clear edges and boundaries. When an architect starts to design a house, he does not yet clearly see all the spaces, fireplaces, windows, doors, and walls. He sees a vision—an optimistic vision of what it will look like when all of the details are in place.

An artist has a vision of a picture before he ever puts brush to canvas. A sculptor would have a vision of what could emerge from a large piece of rock or marble. As we walk it out day to day, we release the destiny we initially saw inside ourselves. These visions are formed before the technical work of developing art is ever started. Sometimes these visions exist as rough pencil sketches. In some artists' exhibits, the gallery will include some of these sketches alongside the finished pieces of art. It is quite remarkable how the early conception turns into a breathtaking—even inspiring—work of creative art.

Why do we need a vision? Because it keeps us focused on direction and on our desires. It is a way to see the future before you actually get to it. God wants you to see your future as He sees it so you will begin to move toward it.

I like to ride bicycles. Sometimes I ride what they call mountain bikes. They are bikes that are built to go off-road and bump around in the dirt. One of the key things you have to quickly learn about riding mountain bikes is you don't look at the big rock that you don't want to hit. You look at the path where you want to go; don't look where you don't want to go. That's easier said than done. You're bombing down the trail and just cooking along. Suddenly, you see this big root sticking up, or a big rock, or a broken bottle in the middle of the trail; your natural inclination is to look at that, focus on that. You think, *I don't want to hit that. I really want to avoid that.* That is the thing that grabs your attention, and sure enough you run right over it. It is very difficult not to look at the obstacle but look where you really want to go instead.

It's like driving down the freeway at night and someone is coming at you with bright lights. If you're not careful you will look at the bright lights. They grab your attention and you start veering toward the oncoming traffic. You will naturally gravitate toward whatever you focus on.

People don't realize that by focusing on their problems, focusing on the things they don't want in life, they are actually moving toward them. Subconsciously, slowly, but in reality, you are moving toward that thing which you focus on. If you focus on what you don't like, what you don't want and what you hope doesn't happen, you are on your way toward it. That's why so many people raised in abusive, alcoholic, drug-using, or angry, sarcastic homes grow up despising the way their family lived. Yet, when they are thirty, forty or fifty years old, they wake up one day and realize they have become the very thing that they didn't want to become.

You don't win games by trying not to lose; you win games by focusing on how to win. You don't become the person you want to be by focusing on the person you don't want to be. Where you focus is so important.

A lot of people really want to lose weight, but they are not doing it. A lot of people really want to make more money, but they are not doing it. So the issue isn't what you want. The issue is where you are focused.

If you focus on your indebtedness, your pain, or your problems, you unconsciously move toward them. It is an unfortunate truth that people usually do not change because they can't see anything else for their lives other than the problems they currently have.

Sometimes we say to ourselves, "I could never see myself living in that house or driving that car." If you have those kind of thoughts, you have limited yourself before you ever start. If you can't see yourself doing something, it is very likely that you will never be able to do it.

I was talking with a guy recently who had gone through a company downsizing. He made it through the downsizing and was still employed there, but he did not know how to feel. He said, "I feel good that I am still employed, but I feel bad about all the people who are unemployed."

I said, "You have to stop that whole mentality."

That is a very common thing. People, in so many ways, are schizophrenic in their thinking. "I'm just glad I have a job, but I feel bad about all those who don't." Move away from that. Get focused. Be glad you have a job, period. We care about people; we love people; and when we have the opportunity, we help and support people. But I can't walk around feeling sorry and responsible for you all day long and still do what I am supposed to be doing with my life.

As you develop your vision of the future, be sure it is what God has called you to and not some worldly desire of the flesh. In fact, some people's lives are so overloaded with stress and complexity that their vision of change should be to move toward simplicity. That is all right if it is a true vision of yours and what God is calling you to. Many are trying to be what parents, teachers, or others want them to be instead of what God has put in their heart.

Change is very desirable if it moves us toward our desires and visions. Keep the faith in your ability to create your future with God's help.

Now take a few minutes and think about your life as it could be when God gives you the desires of your heart.

1. What will it look like?
2. What will be different?
3. What will it feel like?

So far we have discussed two of the key thoughts in bringing about change: desire and vision. To a degree, these are seen from a human perspective. Now, however, let's discuss what God plans for us. This we call *destiny*.

DESTINY: What has God planned for you?

God had planned a wonderful life for you even before He made the earth. Ephesians 1:3–6 says, "Blessed be the God and Father of our Lord Jesus Christ, who has blessed us with every spiritual blessing in the heavenly places in Christ, just as He chose us in Him before the foundation of the world, that we should be holy and without blame before Him in love, having predestined us to adoption as sons by Jesus Christ to Himself, according to the good pleasure of His will, to the praise of the glory of His grace, by which He made us accepted in the Beloved." Knowing your gifts, talents and, most importantly, your desires, He established a destiny for you. He will not take control of your life; you are a free-will agent made in His likeness and image. He made His plan based on your will and desires (Romans 8:29). But He has set a path, a course that is the most exciting, rewarding and fulfilling life that you could ever find.

In your heart you have a sense of what that destiny is. As a Christian, you have a witness of the Spirit as to God's will and plan for you. As you unite with your desires, you will discover your course of destiny.

Here are questions to help you sort out what God has called you to. I pray you will have a spirit of wisdom and revelation in the knowledge of God; the eyes of your understanding being enlightened that you will know the hope of your calling (Eph. 1:17–18). The Holy Spirit will help you know your destiny as you think about and answer these questions:

1. What is the deepest desire of your heart? (Ps. 37:4)
2. What stirs your passion? (John 2:17)
3. What flows naturally out of you? (Rom. 12:4–6)
4. Where do you bring forth fruit or produce good results? (Matt. 12:33)
5. What do mature Christians see in you? (Prov. 11:14)
6. What career or ministry do you feel the peace of God about pursuing? (Col. 3:15 AMP)
7. What thoughts, visions or dreams are impossible to put out of your mind? (Acts 2:17)

8. To what can you give 100 percent of yourself for your entire life? (I Tim. 4:15)
9. What do people want to gather around and help you accomplish? (Matt. 18:19)

Diligently review these three words—*desire, vision,* and *destiny*—and the answers you have found inside yourself for each area. Think about them, rewrite them, and change them as you feel you should. These are the first steps of change toward the fulfillment of your destiny. With desires, vision, and a sense of destiny alive in your heart and mind, you are on your way to a higher level of life. Let the power of God's Word work in you, and see what growth and change begins to happen inside.

DAILY STEPS FOR MEDITATION

Step 1

Psalm 37:4—Delight yourself also in the LORD, and *He shall give you the desires of your heart.*

Question: Do you delight in the Lord? That is, do you find real enjoyment in simply being with Him? If not, why not?

Question: Can you trust God to give you the desires of your heart?

Question: Will the three things you want changed in your life move you toward destiny?

PERSONAL NOTES: ______________________________

____

____

____

____

____

____

____

____

____

____

____

____

____

____

Step 2

Luke 10:38–42—Now it happened as they went that He entered a certain village; and a certain woman named Martha welcomed Him into her house. And she had a sister called Mary, who also sat at Jesus' feet and heard His word. But Martha was distracted with much serving, and she approached Him and said, "Lord, do You not care that my sister has left me to serve alone? Therefore tell her to help me." And Jesus answered and said to her, "Martha, Martha, *you are worried and troubled about many things. But one thing is needed, and Mary has chosen that good part, which will not be taken away from her.*"

Question: Do you feel pressure to always be busy doing something, so that your desires are ignored and your vision is never allowed to develop?

Question: Who are the people in your life that seem to be keeping you occupied? And who are the people that help you move forward in destiny?

Question: How could you rearrange your priorities to find more time to be with Jesus and to do the things He has called you to?

Personal notes: ______________________________

____

____

____

____

____

____

Step 3

Mark 11:24 (KJV)—Therefore I say unto you, *What things soever ye desire*, when ye pray, believe that ye receive them, and ye shall have them.

Question: Do you have specific desires so you can pray with faith and focus?

Question: What experiences or teaching make it hard for you to expect your prayers to be answered?

Question: If you really believe you have received the answer to your prayer, how would you feel, act, etc.?

PERSONAL NOTES: ______________________________

Step 4

Mark 10:51–52—So Jesus answered and said to him, "*What do you want Me to do for you?*" The blind man said to Him, "Rabboni, that I may receive my sight." Then Jesus said to him, "*Go your way; your faith has made you well.*" And immediately he received his sight and followed Jesus on the road.

Question: Do you know what you desire God to do for you, or are you asking what you think you *should* ask?

Question: Are your requests to God steeped in faith or are they just wishes you don't expect to come to pass?

Question: If Jesus asked you today: "What do you want me to do for you?" would you have a clear, meaningful answer for Him?

PERSONAL NOTES: ______________________________

____
____
____
____
____
____
____
____
____
____
____
____

Step 5

Acts 2:17–18—And it shall come to pass in the last days, says God, that I will pour out of My Spirit on all flesh; *your sons and your daughters shall prophesy, your young men shall see visions, your old men shall dream dreams*. And on my menservants and on My maidservants *I will pour out My Spirit* in those days; and they shall prophesy.

Question: What do you dream about when you are awake?

Question: Can you see that your daydreams may be a way to recognizing your desires?

Question: As a matter of self-discipline, can you separate your positive desires from idle, destructive lusts and fantasies?

PERSONAL NOTES: ____________________________________

____

____

____

____

____

____

____

____

____

____

____

____

____

____

Step 6

Habakkuk 2:2–3—Then the LORD answered me and said: "*Write the vision and make it plain* on tablets, that he may run who reads it. For the vision is yet for an appointed time; but at the end it will speak, and it will not lie. Though it tarries, wait for it; because it will surely come, it will not tarry."

Question: Will you write your vision, and not be afraid to make changes as you move forward?

Question: Could you begin to share your dreams with a trusted advisor, such as a pastor or friend, to help refine them into an improved vision of your next level?

Question: What are you beginning to see for your future?

PERSONAL NOTES: ______________________________

____

____

____

____

____

____

____

____

____

____

____

____

____

Step 7

Ephesians 1:11—In Him also we have obtained an inheritance, *being predestined according to the purpose of Him who works all things according to the counsel of His will*, that we who first trusted in Christ should be to the praise of His glory.

Question: What do you sense God has put in your heart as a part of His predestined plan for you?

Question: How does your vision enable you to declare "the praise of His glory"?

Question: In what ways can you act more confidently, having received an inheritance from God Himself?

PERSONAL NOTES: ______________________________

Staying on Course

MEDITATE: **As you focus your thoughts on what you want and where you are going, you will begin to move toward it.**

Let's break some old habits of thinking. Proverbs 23:7 tells us, "As a man thinks in his heart so is he." You are in your current situation because of the way you think about certain things. You get stuck in those circumstances because the same thoughts continue to dominate your mind. We can't change our thinking by trying not to think about something. We change our thinking by focusing on new thoughts and developing a new way of thinking.

In II Corinthians 10:4, the apostle Paul tells us that we are in a battle against strongholds. These can be and are in the mind, in a private battleground. This stronghold is that place where the enemy is able to continue his fight and not be defeated. It is usually camouflaged, hidden, and kept secret so he can continue to wage war. Many of the attitudes which keep us from attaining God's destiny for our lives are in this stronghold.

This enemy—our negative thoughts and temptations toward mediocrity—gains control over our lives because of lazy thoughts, confusion, and keeping the door open to them. It is marked by or exhibits features such as hostility, that cannot be deemed positive or constructive.

If the thought *I am fat* can get a stronghold, it can bring depression, anorexia, bulimia, and even early death. If the thought *I am stupid* gains a stronghold in your mind, it can cause you to drop out of school, give up your dreams, and live in poverty and failure.

Worst of all, if the thought *I can't change* gets a stronghold in your mind, then every aspect of your destiny can be hindered. We have already seen the danger of allowing this thought to control our thinking and lives.

Staying on Course

The person who wants to lose weight must change his thoughts about food and exercise. However, you can't do that by taking a diet pill or trying fad diets. You must develop a new way of thinking about food—why you eat, when you eat, and what you eat—and new thoughts about exercise so you can change and be fit.

Meditation is something you do every day. We all meditate, but we usually don't think about what we're thinking about. We spend hours thinking about what we don't like or don't want in our lives, but we don't meditate on what we do want and what we will like. Remember, whatever you focus your thoughts on you begin to move toward.

Depression and discouragement must be driven out with new hope in God for us to move forward in life. There are three ways we refill our hearts with hope:

1. We get our thoughts off our problems and onto the Lord who solves problems. The message of Joshua 1:6–8 is, "Don't look to the right or the left." That is, keep your focus on the job at hand. "Meditate (focus your thoughts) on the Word of God and you will prosper and have good success."
2. Dream about the things the Lord put into your heart when you first walked with Him. Remember your visions and dreams. Look for ways to take a small step toward those dreams and hopes.
3. Rejoice, praise, and worship God for the hope of your future (Jer. 29:11). Remember the joy of the Lord is your strength (Neh. 8:10), but depression brings weakness.

Remind yourself to think about what you want to change and how your life is altering and transforming. Don't try *not to* think about the things that are wrong or bad. Just think about the things you desire and how life will be when it's changed.

For example: Don't think about being overweight or feeling fat. Focus your thoughts on your vision, how you will look and feel as you change.

To meditate is to ponder, imagine, think about and chew on mentally. While you drive, as you eat, or when you have a spare moment, meditate on your desires, visions and destiny.

DAILY STEPS FOR MEDITATION

Step 8

Ephesians 1:3–6—Blessed be the God and Father of our Lord Jesus Christ, who has blessed us with every spiritual blessing in the heavenly places in Christ, just as *He chose us in Him before the foundation of the world*, that we should be holy and without blame before Him in love, *having predestined us to adoption as sons by Jesus Christ* to Himself, according to the good pleasure of His will, to the praise of the glory of His grace, by which He made us accepted in the Beloved.

Question: What are a few spiritual blessings with which you believe you are especially blessed?

Question: What are some ways that you can become more "holy and without blame before Him"?

Question: Can you take comfort in the fact that the Lord Himself wishes to develop your life as He sees fit?

PERSONAL NOTES: ____________________________________

____
____
____
____
____
____
____
____

Step 9

Ephesians 1:10–11—. . . that in the dispensation of the fullness of the times He might gather together in one all things in Christ, both which are in heaven and which are on earth—in Him. *In Him also we have obtained an inheritance, being predestined according to the purpose* of Him who works all things according to the counsel of His will.

Question: Do you understand that many times, when God seems to be saying "No," He is really saying "Wait"?

Question: What are some things that you can do, that prove God's desire for your life is important to you?

Question: How might you pray for God's perfect will in your life?

PERSONAL NOTES: ______________________________

____

____

____

____

____

____

____

____

____

____

____

____

Step 10

Ephesians 2:10—For we are His workmanship, *created in Christ Jesus for good works, which God prepared beforehand that we should walk in them.*

Question: Is it comforting to you to know that God has personally created us for His pleasure and intentions?

Question: What kind of creative workmanship do you see yourself becoming?

Question: Are you willing to aggressively and consistently seek to discover the paths God has already created for you to walk in?

Personal notes: ______________________________

Step 11

Romans 8:29–32—*For whom He forenew, He also predestined to be conformed to the image of His Son*, that He might be the firstborn among many brethren. *Moreover whom He predestined, these He also called*; whom He called, these He also justified; and whom He justified, these He also glorified. What then shall we say to these things? *If God is for us, who can be against us?* He who did not spare His own Son, but delivered Him up for us all, *how shall He not with Him also freely give us all things?*

Question: Do you feel called by God to do great things in His name?

Question: Do you firmly believe that, for yourself, the power and support of God stands against all things?

Question: What would you ask right now if you knew it satisfied both your desire and God's plan?

Personal notes: ______________________________

____
____
____
____
____
____
____
____
____
____

Step 12

Joshua 1:8—This Book of the Law shall not depart from your mouth, but you shall meditate in it day and night, that you may observe to do according to *all that is written in it. For then you will make your way prosperous, and then you will have good success.*

Question: Is study and meditation in the Bible a living, necessary part of your life every day?

Question: What would fulfill your personal self-image of being prosperous?

Question: What do you think is meant by the term "good success"?

PERSONAL NOTES: ______________________________

____
____
____
____
____
____
____
____
____
____
____
____
____
____
____

Step 13

I Timothy 4:15—*Meditate on these things; give yourself entirely to them*, that your progress may be evident to all.

Question: Do you find it hard to meditate? Perhaps even consider it wasted time?

Question: What are the barriers in your life to serious, regular meditation with the Lord?

Question: What is keeping you from tearing down these barriers, one by one, until you feel entirely sold out to Jesus?

Personal notes: ______________________________

Step 14

> Psalm 1:1–3—Blessed is the man who walks not in the counsel of the ungodly, nor stands in the path of sinners, nor sits in the seat of the scornful; but *his delight is in the law of the LORD, and in His law he meditates day and night*. He shall be like a tree planted by the rivers of water, that brings forth its fruit in its season, whose leaf also shall not wither; and *whatever he does shall prosper*.

Question: Do you see any clues to the barriers to active prayer and meditation in the company you keep?

Question: Are there any relationships which you may have to break to move closer to God?

PERSONAL NOTES: ______________________________

____
____
____
____
____
____
____
____
____
____
____
____
____
____
____
____

The Halfway Point

Now you have examined and meditated on the biblical view of desire, vision and destiny. Hopefully, you have begun to shape and perhaps modify the answers you originally gave to the questions about what you want to change and accomplish in your life.

You have a sense—perhaps limited—of what can be in your life and how you can move to the next level. Yet you need to attain a way of transforming the vision and destiny into something concrete. From this point on, you will be guided to find these answers.

KNOWLEDGE: **You must know the right things to accomplish the right things. Lack of knowledge will keep you from success.**

The prophet Hosea tells us that many of God's people are cut off from blessings because of a lack of knowledge. When we don't know the truths of God that bring success in life, we struggle and eventually fail.

The Halfway Point

Most of us function off the knowledge we received as kids from parents, school, religion and society. We must examine what we believe and think. If these are not in line with God's Word, this may be keeping us from God's will and God's best.

This is limited information, and so many of us try to function with only this. Knowledge, other than what God chooses to give us directly, comes from outside. It is information that has been accumulated, digested, and proclaimed. Getting new information renews the subconscious and enriches the meditation which lets us realize our visions and recognize our destinies.

You have to deepen, study, learn, and plug in to what is available. Read, listen to tapes (even while you drive), hear sermons and mature teachers, and go to seminars and classes. These opportunities increase your knowledge in various areas.

Here's an example. I was raised without much instruction in eating right. So I said, "I don't need breakfast; I don't like it, and I feel better if I don't have it." But then around 10:00 or 11:00 A.M., my blood sugar would get very low, even though I was trying to use my brain full tilt. Then I would eat and hope that my blood sugar level would catch up with my activity needs.

I read a great book on the subject—*Eat Well Live Well*, by Pamela M. Smith—and the author addressed everything that I said about why I did not eat breakfast. She also described what would happen if I changed my habits. Since I read that book, it has changed and improved my abilities greatly. It was knowledge that released a false attitude from my subconscious.

I have believed the wrong things at times, and it has cost me dearly. I thought I was right, but I lacked knowledge, and sure enough I was wrong. It cost me because I had blurred vision due to lack of knowledge.

Expanding your knowledge will do at least two things. First, you will have more raw materials to draw on when you are trying to move to the next level. Second, your meditative experiences will be richer because they can process more.

The brain can hold a lot more than any of us can download. It makes connections between facts and knowledge all the time. Sometimes there is an unanswered concern in our minds, just waiting for the right information to come along and bring satisfaction, relief, and growth. The more we know, the less we will yield to fear, frustration, and fumbling ideas.

Faith: **Believe in yourself and believe in God to enable you to succeed.**

With assurance we can say that if you believe in yourself and believe in God, you will be enabled to succeed. Faith comes by hearing the Word of God (Rom. 10:17). As we learn God's Word, faith will rise in our hearts. Confidence, trust, and faith in God are necessary to receive anything from Him. Things don't happen just because God wants them to happen. We must walk by faith, not by sight (II Cor. 5:7).

Jesus said over and over again, "Your faith has made you whole," and, "According to your faith be it unto you." If you will believe, God will go to work to bring change, renewal, healing, and blessings in your life.

One way of looking at the results of considering our destiny is to have *hope*. Hope can exist on the lower levels of our existence but will fade away if nothing develops from it.

What is needed to let hope guide us to the next level is *faith*. Hebrews 11:1 says, ". . . faith is the substance of things hoped for. . ." See the difference? Hope is ideas in the mind. Faith is substance. What is substance? That which has mass and occupies space; matter. Substance almost always means something touchable. So faith puts a body on our dreams.

Faith is usually thought of as the attitude of absolute belief which assures a personal relationship with Jesus Christ, and a promise of eternal reward. And so it is. Without faith in God, there could be no discovery of personal destiny.

Yet there is a dimension of faith which is directed toward the self. Many people lack this faith in self and thus live at a very low level of attainment.

The tenth chapter of Hebrews mentions many heroes of faith. One of the most interesting is Abraham. Abraham was a moderately successful shepherd in Ur of the Chaldees, but we might see him as living at a low level of achievement. We could imagine, if we try, that he had dreams of something greater and more interesting.

His destiny was completely changed when he followed God's instruction to get up and go, even though he was not told exactly where. Ultimately, his faith led him through many adventures, not always successfully. At the end of his life, however, he was remembered as the father of a mighty nation. By faith he moved to a new level and almost certainly achieved things beyond his wildest dreams.

Begin to believe that God is at work right now answering your prayers, fulfilling your hopes and bringing your vision to pass. Don't think, "It might happen someday." Believe that God is bringing it to pass today!

Perhaps you are not used to thinking this way. You may have a "maybe" attitude in your prayer life, rather than a confident one. If you want your dreams to be achieved, you need to change that to assurance. This may take practice. You will have to keep on thinking about having a positive attitude, but eventually it will become a habit, a part of your nature. Then you can approach God with the certainty that He will respond to your faith.

DAILY STEPS FOR MEDITATION

Step 15

Hosea 4:6—*My people are destroyed for lack of knowledge.* Because you have rejected knowledge, I also will reject you from being priest for Me; because you have forgotten the law of your God, I also will forget your children.

Question: Do you feel like a person who knows very little, or have you been able to learn much?

Question: As you ask God to give you a spirit of discernment to avoid knowledge that either gives place to the enemy or actually causes negativity, what are some areas that you already know you need to avoid?

PERSONAL NOTES: ______________________________

Step 16

> Romans 12:2—And do not be conformed to this world, *but be transformed by the renewing of your mind*, that you may prove what is that good and acceptable and *perfect will of God.*

Question: What are the forces around you that keep you conformed to this world?

Question: What areas of your mind need to be renewed right now if you are to have faith to move forward?

Question: Will you make a commitment right now to daily read more of your Bible, weekly attend church services, monthly join a home meeting, and take in more scriptural teaching tapes and books?

PERSONAL NOTES: ______________________________

Step 17

> Ephesians 4:22–24—. . . that you put off, concerning your former conduct, the old man which grows *corrupt* according to the deceitful lusts, and be renewed in the spirit of your mind, and that you *put on the new man* which was created according to God, in true righteousness and holiness.

Question: Have you learned how to recognize deceitful lusts, those which will not only keep you where you are, but are liable to move you backward?

Question: Based on the knowledge you have or knowledge you are gaining, what is the new man?

Question: In what ways can you actually "put on the new man"?

PERSONAL NOTES: ______________________________

____

____

____

____

____

____

____

____

____

____

____

____

Step 18

Colossians 3:1–2—If then you were raised with Christ, *seek those things which are above*, where Christ is, sitting at the right hand of God. *Set your mind on things above, not on things on the earth.*

Question: What are the things that are above?

Question: How do you benefit from picturing Christ positioned, right there at one with God?

Question: How do you determine what is from above and what is of the earth?

Personal notes: ______________________________

Step 19

Mark 11:22–24—So Jesus answered and said to them, "*Have faith in God*. For assuredly, I say to you, whoever says to this mountain, 'Be removed and be cast into the sea,' and *does not doubt in his heart*, but believes that those things he says will be done, *he will have whatever he says*. Therefore I say to you, whatever things you ask when you pray, *believe that you receive them, and you will have them*."

Question: Is there any other that you are giving your faith, your wholehearted trust, more than God?

Question: Are you becoming better at recognizing your doubts about God or yourself when they creep in to destroy your security?

Question: What is the thing which you would ask for if you dared believe that it would be yours?

PERSONAL NOTES: ______________________________

Step 20

Matthew 8:5–10, 13—Now when Jesus had entered Capernaum, a centurion came to Him, pleading with Him, saying, "Lord, my servant is lying at home paralyzed, dreadfully tormented." And Jesus said to him, "I will come and heal him." The centurion answered and said, "Lord, I am not worthy that You should come under my roof. *But only speak a word*, and my servant will be healed. For I also am a man under authority, having soldiers under me. And I say to this one, 'Go,' and he goes; and to another, 'Come,' and he comes; and to my servant, 'Do this,' and he does it." When Jesus heard it, He marveled, and said to those who followed, "Assuredly, I say to you, I have not found such great faith, not even in Israel!" . . . Then Jesus said to the centurion, "Go your way; and *as you have believed, so let it be done for you.*" And his servant was healed that same hour.

Question: Do you feel comfortable going to God when there is a crisis situation in your life?

Question: Are you developing a feeling of being constantly in the presence of God, hearing Him, sensing Him, and honoring Him?

Question: Is your faith becoming stronger that God will support, guide, and lead you in the destiny He has shown you?

Personal notes: ______________________________

____

____

____

Step 21

Hebrews 11:1–3, 6—Now *faith is the substance of things hoped for, the evidence of things not seen*. For by it the elders obtained a good testimony. By faith we understand that the worlds were framed by the word of God, so that the things which are seen were not made of things which are visible. . . . But *without faith it is impossible to please Him*, for he who comes to God must believe that He is, and that *He is a rewarder of those who diligently seek Him*.

Question: What do you believe is the meaning of "the evidence of things not seen"?

Question: Have you spent too much time trying to please God without really believing Him faithfully?

Question: What do you see as rewards that God will give you for seeking Him?

PERSONAL NOTES: ______________________________

Getting Close

Everything that we have studied and meditated on until now has led you in a positive direction. Hopefully, you have opened your eyes to your desires, developed a vision, and come to at least a beginning understanding of God's destiny for you. You should acknowledge and expect growth as you continue to study.

You have seen the value of knowledge and the twin beliefs—in God and yourself. By answering, in your own words, the questions that have been asked, you have sharpened your idea of what comes next. You are, if you have truly gotten closer to God, excited, poised to move to the next level, leaving behind the old level of comfort.

Still, you may be hesitating. There is something nagging at you, and it is familiar. It is the tendency you have always had to say, "Yeah, but I know it's not going to work." You have started on this program of self-improvement and

Getting Close

that one; you have invested money in things that didn't work out; you have sent resources to a television preacher who just didn't come through for you.

So, now you hesitate.

Here is where the hesitation comes from—a four-letter word: *fear.*

Everyone feels fear at times, such as when confronted by a threatening person or when about to take an exam (especially one not prepared for). The fear I am talking about is the kind that we feel when we have to turn our back on the very comfortable life we have accepted for ourselves and go into a potentially exciting, but unknown, way of doing things.

Whatever causes us fear, it is a big hindrance to change. Fear is a strong emotion and powerful force. It causes people to do things they don't like or want to do. Fear causes people to stay in relationships they don't like and in jobs they hate. It can change the color of a person's hair, eat up a stomach, and destroy health. It brings about changes in the sound of a person's voice.

This strong emotion is caused by the anticipation of something negative. For some reason, human beings are very good at anticipating the negative. We are not talking about a reasonable listing of the possible barriers which can be solved. We are talking about just looking ahead, seeing the bad that you think is going to happen, and letting the emotional feeling of seeing that bad thing affect you right now.

As was said earlier, you may be held back in your desire to become a more fulfilled person by that old familiar feeling of fear. Yet I hope that you are so filled with the possibility of positive change that you are willing to just step over the threshold of your fear and move on out.

To help you see what you may be fearing, I want to mention four types of fear.

Fear of Change

Fear of change is most clearly the fear that affects us in terms of what this book is all about. It is being uncomfortable with anything or anyone that is new or different.

Anything that causes you to pull back from what is different, from what is new, to stay in your current circumstances—though not what you want—feels better than the pain and discomfort of change.

This fear may extend from reluctance to change the desk we have always worked at, to the kind of person we have always gravitated to in a relationship. Also, you may always be *planning* to make changes, but the plans themselves become the method to avoid change. Here are some words that may sound familiar:

- "I'm going to . . ."
- "I'm in the process . . ."
- "I'm getting the money to redo the home."
- "I'm in the process of moving to a different . . ."

You may be in a church or denomination that just does not satisfy you, but there you stay. You don't "get anything out of going," but you remain. You may have been baptized there, or you just feel comfortable being able to say you are a Lutheran, a Catholic, a Baptist, or whatever. If you are honest, the reason is that the pain and discomfort of having to find something new and different—and better—is just too scary.

Let me tell you a personal story. A friend called me and asked me to go hunting. I'd never been hunting. When I was sixteen I shot a squirrel and cried—that was the closest to hunting I had ever done. So I said, "Yeah, okay, I'll go." I was thinking, "Okay, I'm going to walk through the woods and get branches in my hair." But I hunted for the first time, had a great time, and it opened up a whole new realm. It opened up new relationships, new activities, and new things I could do with my son. If I hadn't done something I'd never done, I would have missed a whole lot of opportunities I never knew were there.

I've heard there is an old sign in the foothills of the Appalachians that says, "Choose your rut wisely—you'll be in it for the next 160 miles." You may be in yours for the rest of your life if you don't let the power of God usher you past the artificial barrier of your fear of change.

Now, we will talk more about three other types of fear that you may experience regularly or from time to time.

Fear of Failure

How many great relationships never got started because one was afraid to go ask for the first date? "What if she says no?" She might as well have said no—you didn't get the date!

The ironic thing is that fear of failure produces the very thing you're afraid is going to happen. That's why it has such power. It brings about in our lives the very thing that we're afraid that it's going to bring about.

You find a self-fulfilling prophecy here. You say, "I knew it wouldn't work." "How did you know that?" "Well, I didn't try, but I knew it wouldn't." You were right. You didn't try and you didn't succeed, and your prophecy was fulfilled.

Fear of Success

It sounds strange to say that someone can be afraid of success. Most people who suffer from this fear probably don't even realize it. They think their problems and limitations come from somewhere else.

Fear of success is rooted in the concern that if a person goes to the next level, and achieves prosperity or whatever he thinks is his destiny, he will have responsibilities that he now does not. People will expect things of him!

As long as you are barely getting by, you can say, "Hey, what can I do? It's not my fault! Why, if I had the resources, you know I'd do something!"

God does not accept that excuse. He says, "No, that's not true. I gave you a living; you didn't use it. I gave you life; you didn't develop it. You settled for your mediocre, selfish, maintenance lifestyle because you were afraid of success."

It is important for you to look deep within and, with God's help, see if you are gripped with the fear of failure. If you find that this is actually true, you have identified another enemy and can beat it.

Fear of People

You are subject to this fear when you are too concerned with what people think, what they might say, or how they might act. Many people are hindered by this fear. They simply recoil from any conflict, slight, objection, or insult.

The Bible says fear of man is a snare which traps, binds, and holds you back. Strangely, people are the most important thing in our human lives. Almost everyone needs solid relationships and intimacy. Success speakers say that people skills are 90 percent of every job.

What is important is how you feel about those people. To be fully effective, and to move to a better level, you need to become free from care about what they might think, what they might say, or what they might do.

DAILY STEPS FOR MEDITATION

Step 22

Proverbs 3:5–6—*Trust in the LORD with all your heart*, and lean not on your own understanding; in all your ways *acknowledge Him*, and He shall direct your paths.

Question: Is it apparent that your battle with all types of fear begins with trust in God?

Question: In what way can you display your complete trust in Him today?

Question: Is your destiny—the plan you have put together with God—important enough to you to overcome your fear of change?

PERSONAL NOTES: ________________________________

____

____

____

____

____

____

____

____

____

____

____

____

____

Step 23

Psalm 112:6–7—. . . The righteous will be in *everlasting remembrance*. He will *not be afraid of evil tidings*; His heart is steadfast, *trusting in the* LORD.

Question: In overcoming fear, can you draw upon the knowledge that God always remembers you and your situation?

Question: Is there sometimes more to be feared from *tidings*, or imaginary trouble, than there is from a danger right in front of us?

Question: Is there any greater object of your trust than the Lord? If so, is it going to always be there to help?

PERSONAL NOTES: ______________________________

____

____

____

____

____

____

____

____

____

____

____

____

____

____

Step 24

Psalm 118:5–6—I called on the Lord in distress; The Lord *answered me* and set me in a *broad place*. The Lord is on my side; *I will not fear. What can man do to me*?

Question: Do you feel free to call on the Lord when you are distressed?

Question: Are you distressed right now? What about?

Question: Even though you recognize that man can surely damage your body, are you able to see how the Lord can help you see past the dangers that exist only in your mind?

Personal notes: ______________________________

Step 25

Matthew 25:25, 28—And *I was afraid*, and went and hid your talent in the ground. Look, there *you have what is yours*. . . . Therefore *take the talent from him*, and give it to him who has ten talents.

Question: Are you sometimes like the servant who was more afraid of losing his master's money than of expanding it?

Question: Do you occasionally hide behind the notion that God can do whatever He wishes, so you don't have to do anything to make Him happy?

Question: What truly important thing have you lost in your life by letting fear rule your decision-making process?

Personal notes: ______________________________

____
____
____
____
____
____
____
____
____
____
____
____
____

Step 26

Mark 4:39–41—Then He arose and rebuked the wind, and said to the sea, *"Peace, be still!"* And the wind ceased and there was a great calm. But He said to them, *"Why are you so fearful?* How is it that you have no faith?" And they feared exceedingly, and said to one another, *"Who can this be, that even the wind and the sea obey Him!"*

Question: Are you able to sense God calming your enemies to bring you to confidence?

Question: Knowing God's power and His concern for you, do you still cling to fear?

Question: Can you let your familiarity with the natural world fade into awe at God's ultimate power over all internal fears?

PERSONAL NOTES: ______________________________

____
____
____
____
____
____
____
____
____
____
____
____
____

Step 27

> Romans 8:15–16—For you did not receive *the spirit of bondage again to fear*, but you received *the Spirit of adoption* by whom we cry out, "Abba, Father." The Spirit Himself bears witness with our spirit that *we are children of God.*

Question: Do you see that being wrapped up by fear is just as controlling as being in shackles?

Question: Does it give you comfort to know that God has adopted you into His loving care?

Question: In what sense do you feel like a child of God?

PERSONAL NOTES: ____________________

Step 28

John 14:27—"Peace I leave with you. *My peace I give to you*; not as the world gives do I give to you. Let not your heart be troubled, *neither let it be afraid.*

Question: Do you feel a sense of peace in your soul?

Question: What specific things is the world doing to you to rob you of moving more peacefully forward in your life?

Question: Are you ready to step out of your fears into confident thought and action?

Personal notes: ______________________________

Reaching the Summit

In the introduction to this devotional series, it was pointed out that change is difficult for many people. The previous level led us through some of the things we fear and how God is able to help us overcome these fears. As we have gained a vision and have even learned how to obtain knowledge to carry out God's destiny for us, we will confront the fear of change.

Following are thoughts that we need to consider prayerfully to help us overcome the fear of change which otherwise will keep us right where we are—unfulfilled and dissatisfied.

RENEWING: **Old thoughts and habits must be replaced with new thoughts and habits.**

As we learn new scriptures and biblical truth, we must make sure we are renewing and not just gaining knowledge. Learning is part of the process of change, but we must release old, negative thoughts and focus on new thoughts. Take off the old and put on the new.

Renewing the mind is exchanging old ways of thinking for new ways so that you think and believe like Jesus teaches us to. Those who never change will never move in God's will for their lives. The book of Proverbs teaches us that those who will not renew their minds are fools (Prov. 9:7–9).

God told you to be renewed in the spirit of your mind. This implies you *can* renew your mind. Many people don't realize what a tremendous gift God gave each person in the ability to renew your mind. It's not an easy task because your brain was made to lock onto things, hang onto them, and never let them go. But you *can* do it!

We are supposed to raise our children with a positive spirit, to put faith, confidence, and vision into them. They

Reaching the Summit

lock onto it, they never let it go, and when they're old they won't depart from it.

The greatest gift is that there is nothing a human being can't change. Oh, I know you're not going to change your stature, you're not going to change your appearance to a great degree (although you can change your fitness level and health), but you *can* change attitudes, you *can* change outlooks, and you *can* change in the area of how you think and what you do in your career.

This is one of the things you have been meditating on, praying about, and considering for the past several weeks. It is a gift—one you really need to take advantage of.

RELEASE: **You must let go of things that will hold you down and keep you from changing.**

There are and will be many thoughts, beliefs and attitudes that you must release to move ahead in destiny. Letting go of the past, negative thoughts and even negative people is a big part of change. People who will not release these things get stuck in mediocre lives and worldly ruts.

We know what it feels like to release something we've been holding on to. You might have carried a suitcase through a large airport; remember how good your arm and shoulder muscles felt when you put it down? Or perhaps you went deep-sea fishing and had to wrestle with a large sailfish for many minutes, or even an hour. When the fish was finally boated, you were able to relax and you suddenly realized how tired and cramped your hands, arms, and back had been. How good it felt to let go of something.

The mind can also be very fatigued and cramped from holding on to heavy, useless ideas, or to inhibiting notions of what can and can't be done. If you have been around someone who has found spiritual liberation by accepting Christ's promise of eternal life—in spite of all their sins—you have seen how they feel a staggering burden has been removed. They feel like doing a spiritual dance on light feet!

Examine those thoughts, attitudes and people that may stop you from changing and moving ahead with the Lord.

REVIEW: **"Re-view" every step you have taken.**

We don't learn overnight. We learn by going over and over and over new material, attitudes or actions. Don't give up. Go over these things again and get these scriptures in your heart and life.

It has been said that it takes at least twenty-five repetitions of a new practice to turn it into a habit. Most people feel they can't change because they never work on it long enough. Any golfer will tell you that changing a bad swing habit is a real challenge. In fact, golf is one of those sports where practice, practice, practice may do nothing but reinforce bad habits. It takes some top-level professionals a year or more to build a new, more effective swing.

So, likewise, in your spiritual life, as you move to the next level, don't expect it to be done overnight. With God's help, and a decision on your part, you need to continually review, practice, and internalize the new habits which will help you grow.

I encourage you to work through the lessons of this book over and over until the promises in it take over your life!

DAILY STEPS FOR MEDITATION

Step 29

Romans 8:5–6—For those who live according to the flesh set their minds on the things of the flesh, but *those who live according to the Spirit, the things of the Spirit*. For to be carnally minded is death, but to be spiritually minded is life and peace.

Question: Are you increasingly able to discern between the things of the flesh and the things of the Spirit?

Question: How might you go about eliminating those things which hold you back from your full destiny in the Lord?

Question: Are you consistently aggressive in your development of a vision, a destiny, and a full relationship with God?

PERSONAL NOTES: ______________________________

____

____

____

____

____

____

____

____

____

____

Step 30

John 8:31–32—Then Jesus said to those Jews who believed Him, "If you *abide in My word*, you are My disciples indeed. And *you shall know the truth, and the truth shall make you free*."

Question: Do you place a high value on study, memorization, and internalization of scripture?

Question: Is your understanding of your destiny constantly challenged and stretched by your understanding of God as revealed in the Bible?

Question: How have the scriptures you have read in the previous levels helped you to grow to the next level of existence and realization of your destiny?

PERSONAL NOTES: ______________________________

Step 31

Proverbs 4:20–23—My son, *give attention to my words*; incline your ear to my sayings. Do not let them depart from your eyes; *keep them in the midst of your heart*; for *they are life* to those who find them, and health to all their flesh. *Keep your heart* with all diligence, for out of it spring the *issues of life*.

Question: Do you get a sense of renewal from your time spent alone with God, along with His Word?

Question: Do you see how these lessons have led you to the real issues of *your* life?

Question: Might you be helped to grow and strengthen your grasp of your destiny by "re-viewing" the scriptures in this book?

PERSONAL NOTES: ____________________

Step 32

> James 1:22–25—But *be doers of the word*, and not hearers only, deceiving yourselves. For if anyone is a hearer of the word and not a doer, he is like a man observing his natural face in a mirror; for he observes himself, goes away, and immediately forgets what kind of man he was. But *he who looks into the perfect law of liberty* and continues in it, and is not a forgetful hearer but a *doer of the work, this one will be blessed in what he does.*

Question: Is there any danger that you will forget what you learned about your destiny and simply send this to your heap of failures?

Question: Can you see how taking action steps will help you avoid being victimized by the paralysis of analysis?

Question: What specific actions do you need to take to get your life to a level of fulfillment?

PERSONAL NOTES: ______________________________

Step 33

Joshua 1:6–9—*Be strong and of good courage*, for to this people you shall divide as an inheritance the land which I swore to their fathers to give them. Only *be strong and very courageous, that you may observe to do according to all the law* which Moses My servant commanded you; *do not turn from it to the right hand or to the left, that you may prosper wherever you go*. This Book of the Law shall not depart from your mouth, but you shall meditate in it day and night, that you may observe to do according to all that is written in it. *For then you will make your way prosperous, and then you will have good success*. Have I not commanded you? Be strong and of good courage; do not be afraid, nor be dismayed, for the Lord your God is with you wherever you go.

Question: Do you see that even though God provides the possibilities, you must be active, not passive, in achieving your destiny?

Question: How many ways can you define the word *prosperous*?

Question: Do you have lingering doubts that the Lord does not have a concern that you be a prosperous person walking a prosperous way?

Personal notes: ______________________________

____

____

____

____

Step 34

Matthew 18:18–19—Assuredly, I say to you, *whatever you bind on earth will be bound in heaven, and whatever you loose on earth will be loosed in heaven*. Again I say to you that if two of you agree on earth concerning anything that they ask, *it will be done* for them by My Father in heaven.

Question: Is it not an awesome thought and responsibility that God has enabled you to determine some activities even in the heavenlies?

Question: Do you have an experienced, godly mentor who can help you to discover and reverently follow God's destiny for you?

Question: Do you realize that to pray in Jesus' name means to pray in the intentions of the Father?

PERSONAL NOTES: ______________________________

____

____

____

____

____

____

____

____

____

____

____

____

Step 35

I Corinthians 15:58—Therefore, my beloved brethren, *be steadfast, immovable, always abounding in the work of the Lord,* knowing that your labor is not in vain in the Lord.

Question: What does it mean in *your* life to be steadfast and immovable?

Question: How is your destiny compatible with the work of the Lord?

Question: Are you now prepared to go forward to the next level with the knowledge that no labor you make in that effort, in Jesus' name, is in vain?

PERSONAL NOTES: ______________________________

A Final Word

The Christian life is a climb up the mountain of God; the view gets better with every step. It takes desire, drive, discipline, diligence, and determination. This transformation can only happen when you get out of your comfort zone and meet God on a higher level.

Your mountain of transformation can begin with any book (such as this one), a class, activity, service, or relationship that causes you to view things differently and begin to make changes in your normal way of life. Those who never go to the mountain, never see the full glory of God, never receive the full Word of God—they settle for a much lower form of life.

Your vision for your life is worth waiting and working for. Get ready and keep yourself ready to climb and possess your mountain!

To order additional copies please call:

1-800-644-4446

or write to

Christian Faith International
P.O. Box 98800
Seattle, WA 98198